You!

Also available in RED FOX

Turn that Racket Down
Poptastic Poetry edited by Paul Cookson

My Mate Fancies You!

Paul Cookson
Poetry Passions

A Red Fox Book

Published by Random House Children's Books
20 Vauxhall Bridge Road, London SW1V 2SA

A division of The Random House Group Ltd
London Melbourne Sydney Auckland
Johannesburg and agencies throughout the world

1 3 5 7 9 10 8 6 4 2

First published in Great Britain
by Red Fox, 2001

Printed and bound in Great Britain by
Bookmarque Ltd, Croydon, Surrey

THE RANDOM HOUSE GROUP Limited Reg. No. 954009

ISBN 0 09 940964 X

'Serious Luv' by Benjamin Zephaniah first published in *Funky Chickens*
by Viking Books 1996

'Sonnet 4 Sharon' and 'An Item' by David Horner first published in *Body Noises*
by Apple Pie Publications

My Life is Over

My life is over tonight for sure
now that Brenda Barnes has sussed me out,
she'll be telling everyone, no doubt,
how I'm really useless at kissing.

Brenda will broadcast it all round school
so I might as well write my farewell note,
join the Foreign Legion, stowaway on a boat,
now I'm labelled useless at kissing.

I practised in front of the mirror for hours,
puckering up and closing my eyes,
but as from tomorrow I'll be in disguise
when the girls know I'm useless at kissing.

Her lips were like fire, I thought I'd been burned,
I jumped back quickly, she obviously thought
I'd rejected her, now my chances are nought,
someone please help me practise my kissing.

I know that I shouldn't contemplate this
but there's no way out, my senses are numb,
overnight, someone please, strike Brenda dumb
and keep secret that terrible kiss.

Brian Moses

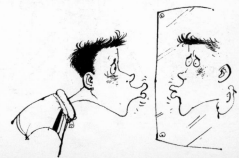

How to Spot a Sister in Love

Spends even longer than usual in the bathroom
borrows Mum's perfume
sits by the telephone all evening
keeps little notes under her pillow
giggles when you mention the boy's name
won't eat anything at all
changes her clothes every twenty minutes
keeps weighing herself
stays up late into the night playing mushy music
is early for school.

How to Spot a Brother in Love

Looks for hairs on his chin to shave
starts missing his football matches
buys aftershave
asks for his shirt to be ironed again
– or even does it himself!
asks his friends if he has spots
cuts his toenails
wants deodorant for his birthday
reads the problem pages in magazines
won't wear odd socks
cleans out his earwax
and is also early for school.

Andrew Collett

Not in Love

I'm not in love, oh no – there's no chance,
Just because I stuck my chewing gum in your hair.
Don't think I fancy you because
You sometimes find me sitting in your chair.

Don't think that I'm in love with you because
When you get answers right, I call you swot.
When I pinch your pen or break your ruler
Don't take that for affection, 'cause it's not.

Don't think it bothers me that I don't see you
When we're in separate sports halls for P.E.
When we're apart on Saturday and Sunday
Don't think it makes a difference to me.

If I get awkward when I see you crying
Or linger just a little at the bell,
You'll understand it's not because I like you –
Unless I find that you like me as well.

Richard Hazlehurst

A Gift for What's-'is-Name

I've taken out me chewing gum.
Can I give it to thingummy, Miss?
I'm in love with 'im cos 'e wipes 'is nose
On 'is sleeve before we kiss.
And none of the other boys I know
Are quite as polite as this.

Nick Toczek

First Kisses

First kisses are worrying,
I mean, what do you do?
And is there a right way of doing it?

Do you keep your lips dead tight
and rub them side to side?
Or do you leave them open
and let them go all squishy and wobbly?

Should you do sink plunger impressions?

Is it safer to leave them open –
at least until you know
that you're not going to bang noses?

What happens if both your glasses steam up
at the same time?
Or your braces get caught in theirs?

What about if you dribble?

Be careful if you sneeze . . .
you might blow their head off.
And what happens if . . .
you breathe in suddenly?

Whatever you do – and whoever you do it with –
just remember this one very important rule:
Make sure that the first person you ever ever kiss
Does not have a runny nose.

Paul Cookson

Penny and Kathryn

Penny and Kathryn
that year they seemed older
though we were all ten.
I'd watch them in class,
they didn't chatter or laugh,
were so calm at their work
it made me feel nervous.
Gawky Penny seemed now to be
slim and clever, her new glasses
made her eyes large and dreamy
above the small pout of her mouth.
Kathryn was stocky, strong,
her thick hair shook as she moved
always as if sure where she was going:
I liked that energy, almost feared it.

I wasn't mooning over them, they were just
more interesting than the other girls,
somehow stronger than the boys.
I would have liked to be friends with them.

But one warm evening, going home,
we saw them behind us on the road,
two other boys and me, we said,
let's hide, let's jump out, it's fun –
we thought it friendly, meant no harm.
And I hid behind a gate post like the others,
enjoying the wait, the tension,
and leapt up grinning, happy as a puppy.

But the girls didn't look surprised
or laugh or run or anything:
they just looked, and the looks
said they were past that sort of game,
that we were silly little boys, to be ignored,
and they left me standing foolish by the wall
feeling they were right and knowing,
even as I made a rude face to cover up my shame,
how big a gap there was between us
that I couldn't cross until I learnt
what different games would please them.

Dave Calder

21

Down in the Dumps

You know James,
Gentle James?
The boy with spiky orange hair who's ace at games?
I dumped him.

You know Mark,
Mad bad Mark?
The boy who cuddled Kirsten during Murder
in the Dark?
I dumped him.

You know Glenn,
Gorgeous Glenn?
The boy Pip's had a thing for since I don't know when.
I dumped him.

You know Jake,
Jokey Jake?
The boy who fools around with Kate and Jessica
at break.
I dumped him.

You know Steve,
Shirt-off Steve?
The boy who's got a build you just would not believe.
I dumped him.

You know Des,
Desperate Des?
The boy who paid ten quid to see Sam's chest,
or so she says?
I dumped him.

I dumped them all
For little Paul.
I can't recall this Paul at all.
He dumped me.

John Whitworth

Medical Complaint?

Tommy said girlfriends were like tonsillitis.
'But why?' asked his puzzled mate, Fred.
'If you'd had the same ones as I've had,
you'd know –
They're a pain in the neck!' Tommy said . . .

Clive Webster

After Words

Sitting
on a
swing,
thinking,
'Wish you
were here,
pushing.'

Mike Johnson

Serious Luv

Monday morning

I really luv de girl dat's sitting next to me
I think she thinks like me an she's so cool,
I think dat we could live for ever happily
I want to marry her when I leave school.

She's de only one in school allowed to call me Ben.
When she does Maths I luv de way she chews her pen,
When we are doing Art she's so artistic
In Biology she makes me heartbeat so quick.

When we do Geography I go to paradise
She's helped me draw a map of Borneo twice!
Today she's going to help me take me books home
So I am going to propose to her when we're alone.

The next day

I used to luv de girl dat's sitting next to me
But yesterday it all came to an end,
She said that I should take love more seriously
An now I think I really luv her friend.

Benjamin Zephaniah

Naomi and Wolf

All my mates fancy Naomi.
When she met Wolf
She said, Wow!
What a cool dog.
Oh yeah, I said.
What a size!
Oh yeah, I said.
What's his name?
Wolf.
Hello Wolf, said Naomi,
I had a dog like him once.
Naomi went all wistful,
Remembering something sad,
Something bad.
He got run over, she sighed,
By an articulated truck
Carrying frozen herrings
To Humberside.
Her eyes looked sadder
Than Wolf's.
Can I walk home with you
And Wolf? she asked.
Sure, I said nonchalantly.
To myself I said,
Y-E-S!!!

Roger Stevens

Rachel said – so I did

Rachel said, 'You're very sweet but
I like boys who are
Mysterious,
Lovers of animals,
Good at sport,
Writers of poetry
And blond.'

So, I borrowed
Dad's sunglasses,
Next door's dog,
My brother's football,
Mum's notebook
And my sister's wig.

But when I walked past Rachel's house
With a notebook over my face,
The wig on a lead,
Bouncing the sunglasses,
Scribbling on the ball
And the dog on my head,
Rachel said, 'You're weird.'

John Coldwell

An Item

with no crick
    there's no crack
without a tee
    there's no vee
with no knick
    there's no knack
without you
    there's no me.

with no chop
    there's no stick
without a bam
    there's no boo
with no pic
    there's no nic
without me
    there's no you
with no hedge
    there's no hog
without a fizz
    there's no buzz
with no hot
    there's no dog
without the two
    there's no of us.

David Horner

The Girl I Go Out With . . .

. . . Is not a girl
who pokes me with her skinny fingers
right in the back when she wants to talk,
who has long nails that scratch my arm
and who whispers to her friends
and giggles and gossips
the minute she sees me walking towards her.

So that I go redder than a beetroot
dropped in a bucket of very red paint
and hotter than a firework that fell in the bonfire
so that both my feet suddenly sprout
to twice their size, making me trip up
the exact moment I walk past her
and she puts her hand over her mouth
nudges her mate and cackles,
'Look at him, what a nerd.'

The girl I go out with
is quiet and calm,
she talks to me
about clothes and music,
she doesn't spend her whole life thinking
she's the coolest catwalker on the planet.

David Harmer

The Boy I Go Out With . . .

. . . Is not a boy
who pinches my headband
and pulls my hair, then yells rude words
at the top of his creaking-cracking
up-and-down squeaking voice.

Is not a boy who burps very loudly
at all possible times, who squeezes
and squirts his spots at his mates
as he digs around the caves of his nostrils
for giant bogies to flick at me.

Is not a boy
who mutters and mumbles
under his breath or, even worse,
grunts like a pig each time he speaks,
a lump of chewing gum stuck in his mouth,
his whole body stinking
of hair gel, deodorant, dirty trainers
and cheese and onion crisps.

The boy I go out with
is a boy with a brain.
He talks in sentences,
he wears cool clothes,
doesn't spend his whole life thinking
he's the best snog on the planet.

David Harmer

Animal Magnetism

I was only a wee little sprog
When I had my very first snog
Ten minutes long
All dribbles and tongue . . .
It's a pity it was from my dog!

Paul Cookson

Hopelessly Devoted

Do you fancy Lisa?

> Who? Do you mean Lisa who's got curly, dyed-auburn hair with subtle silvery streaks, deep green eyes that you could dive into like a dolphin, a cute sort-of dimply chin, luscious lips (especially when she's been sucking a strawberry ice-lolly), under a slightly turned-up nose, ears with gold studs, runs like a gazelle, plays wing attack at netball, clever with computers, got a cat called 'Superpuss', supports the same soccer team as me, lives at 41 Lennox Lane, by the bus shelter, phone number 534337 and has two younger sisters?

Yes, that Lisa.

> Can't say I've really noticed her, actually.

Mike Johnson

Once

He's a twit, he's a twerp, he's a wimp, he's a chump.
He's a grouch, he's a growl, he's a grub, he's a grump.
He's a geek, he's a gink, he's a skunk, he's a jerk,
He's a nit, he's a git, he's a brat, he's a berk.
He's a blimp, he's a bozo, a snitch and a snob,
A slouch and a sleaze and a slug and a slob.
He's a crook, he's a crawler, a creep and a crud,
He's a klutz, he's a clod, he's a dolt, he's a dud.

He's an oaf, he's a fruitcake, a nerd and a nut,
He's a boil on your neck and a pain in your gut,
He's a snoop, he's a smarm, he's a snivelling sneak,
He's scraggy and scrawny and woozy and weak.
He's skanky, he's manky, he's stinky, he's smelly,
A dirtbag, a slimebag, a sickbag, a jelly.
He burbles, he babbles, he gurgles, he niggles,
He sniffles, he snuffles, he gabbles, he giggles.

He's squishy, he's squelchy, he's slubbery-slobbery,
Slippery-sloppery, blubbery-blobbery,
Wobbly-waddly, wriggly-fiddly,
Waffly-piffly, dribbly-piddly,
Dweeby, dorky, dopey, dumb,
Drippy, sappy, geeky, crumb,
Fee-fi-fo-fum
FATFACE! FATBUM!

He's the wax in your lughole, the pus in your spot,
He's a bucket of gunge, he's a barrel of snot.
He's a fungus, a virus, a corpse in a coffin,
He once was my boyfriend.
                            (I think I've gone off him.)

John Whitworth

I Knew I Loved Her . . .

She wears baggy pants
and a white lace top to school.
She has ink-black hair,
tied in two pony tails.
She's the quickest in Maths.
She can spell archa . . .
          arhco . . .
          acrho . . .
She can spell lots of big words.
She played the Queen in the school play,
I was her humble servant.
She was elected school captain,
I voted for her (twice!).
She knows the capital of Tanzania.
She knows who invented the telephone.
I ring her home – it's always engaged.
She knows the history of Ancient Egypt.
She knows how flowers grow.
I pick them for her – they die
before I work up the courage.

But after all this
I only realized I loved her
when
during Friday's game
as the ball came across
she pivoted on one leg
and volleyed it into the net
and we won the Final
with that goal
and then,
I was sure,
I knew that I loved her.

Steven Herrick

My Friend Says ...

My friend says she loves you
> *Well I don't feel the same*

She says she thinks you're really cool
> *Well I think she's a pain*

My friend thinks you're handsome
> *Quite frankly I don't care*

She says she dreams of you at night
> *Oh Lord, what a nightmare*

My friend says she wants a date
> *I'd rather end up dead*

My friend's dad's a millionaire
> *I take back all I've said.*

Richard Caley

Mum's Out

Mum's out.
Kev's come round.
Sis is upstairs
so we won't make a sound.

We're holding hands
on the settee,
sitting as close
as we can be.

A quick kiss.
Could be better.
It's awfully hot
in this sweater.

Mum comes in
when we're in a clinch!
'Hold it right there.
Don't move an inch.'

Two red faces.
What will she say?
Caught in the act –
it's not our day.

Jill Townsend

41

It's Me, Over Here ...

'Shall I compare thee to a summer's day?'
is what some poet said.
I'd like to say the same to you
but then I'd go all red

and ride me bike into the wall
and bend back all me teeth
and then you wouldn't fancy me,
so then you'd go with Keith.

But he don't know no poems
and he's got skanky breath
so love with him would taste all sour.
Do you like speccy Jeff?

And then there's Darren. He's too tall,
though he would make you laugh.
To get your lips near his would be
like kissing a giraffe.

42

And after that there's Tommo,
Beezer, Shane and Jack,
a queue of lads and losers
whilst your true love's at the back.

So why do you need to be with those?
They're not the ones for you.
I'll wait for you for ever,
well, until I'm twenty-two.

You are a summer's day to me,
you are a mountain stream.
If football was a game for one
then you'd be my whole team.

So I'm writing you this poem,
forgive the crossings out.
I'm this bottled up, shy twelve year old
whose heart is fizzing out.

Stewart Henderson

I'd Never Fall in Love with a Girl

I'd never fall in love with a *girl*.

I might fall in love with my new tracksuit top
or my bike
or my Mum –
but I'd never fall in love with a *girl*.

I might fall in love with my old casie football
or Liverpool F.C.
or Auntie Sandra
(she's really nice,
but she's grown up,
and anyway she's married to my Uncle Eddie),
but I'd never fall in love with a *girl*.

I might fall in love with Tessa Jones,
but she's not like a girl at all really.
She can run faster,
climb higher, fight harder
and kick a football further
than any of the boys.

I might *even* fall in love
with my mate Stephen
(if he'd let me, that is) –
except he can't run as fast,
or climb as high, or fight as hard,
or kick a ball as far
as Tessa Jones . . .

But I'd *never* fall in love
WITH A GIRL.

Dave Ward

Honesty is ...

He was trying a new line in chat-up –
'You've got the face of a saint.'
'Which one?' she asked, feeling romantic.
'A Saint Bernard,' he said. She felt faint . . .

Clive Webster

When My True Love Dumped Me . . .

Mum, Dad, all my friends, rallied round with sympathy:
'Don't worry! Cheer up!'
        Then they said a phrase most odd:
'Just look on the bright side,
        there's plenty more fish in the sea.'
What a stupid thing to say . . .
        Who wants to snog a cod?

Paul Cookson

i wanna be yours

let me be your vacuum cleaner
breathing in your dust
let me be your Ford Cortina
i will never rust
if you like your coffee hot
let me be your coffee pot
you call the shots
i wanna be yours

let me be your raincoat
for those frequent rainy days
let me be your dreamboat
when you wanna sail away
let me be your teddy bear
take me with you anywhere
i don't care
i wanna be yours

let me be your electric meter
i will not run out
let me be the electric heater
you get cold without
let me be your setting lotion
hold your hair
with deep devotion
deep as the deep
atlantic ocean
that's how deep is my emotion
deep deep deep deep de deep
deep
i don't wanna be hers
i wanna be yours

John Cooper Clarke

Miss You

Dear Kevin,
    Just a line from here -
Miss you, miss you, miss you, dear!
Both sea and sky down here are grey;
So far it's rained all holiday -
Looks like going on for weeks.
Our caravan has fifteen leaks:
It's saturated all our gear.
Kevin, love, wish you were here.
Dad says the beer down here's no good.
The beach has got no sand - just mud;
And what's between us and the sea?
You'll never guess - a cemetery.
My new swimsuit gave Mum a fit:
She says there's not enough of it.
(I'm pretty sure you won't agree:
It does show off a lot of me!)
If you were here to joke and natter
The gloom and doom just wouldn't
                    matter.

Coming with them, it's pretty clear,
Was not a brilliant idea.
Closing now, Kev, I'm off to bed;
Think I've got flu, I feel half dead.
Hoping from this exciting whirl
You're not out with some other girl.
Miss you at Misery-on-Sea,
Love you to bits.

Your girl friend,
G

Eric Finney

It's the Way That You Say It

I don't deserve
Your lack of lerve!
Must I now prove
How much I loove?
Why won't you give
A little liv?
I'm dreaming of
Our secret lov.
Just listen, Kev,
I need your lev.
Now that I have
Fallen in lav.
The spell's gone wrong
In this luv song.

Andrew Fusek Peters

First Love

Sarah's my girlfriend,
Without her I feel
Like a ball with no bounce,
A shoe with no heel,
An up with no down,
A snow with no flake,
A fish trying to swim
In a waterless lake.
Sarah's my girlfriend,
Without her I fear
I feel that I'm nowhere,
Especially not here.

Brian Patten

GONE!

I'll Love You Till . . .

I'll love you till . . .
Mount Everest is an anthill
the Pacific Ocean is a puddle
the Arctic is a hot spring
and polar bears live in the desert.

I'll love you till . . .
pizzas are made of plastic
spaghetti is short and fat
sausages are square
and only eaten on Wednesdays.

I'll love you till . . .
monkeys swing through supermarkets
zebras are stripeless
and people bounce round on their heads
especially on concrete.

I'll love you till . . .
children teach teachers
homework is banned
and schools close every day except Christmas
when nobody goes anyway.

I'll love you till . . . till . . . till . . .
at least next Friday's disco.

Rita Ray

Just to Make Sure

He was feeling just slightly romantic,
He took out a 'lonely hearts' ad.
And joy – he had an enquiry,
Perhaps life wasn't so bad.

They arranged to meet at the station,
He'd get in at six forty-five,
And she'd be there, lovely, excited,
Waiting for him to arrive.

'But darling,' he wrote in his letter,
'There's something I think you should know –
I've got hundreds of pimples and dandruff,
And a nose with a permanent glow.

'I've got two heads and I'm slimy,
I've got three legs and one arm.
Are you sure you still want to meet me?'
He wrote, with increasing alarm.

She wrote back, 'My darling, don't worry,
I'll meet you at six forty-five.
But please, may I ask you a favour
To help me when you arrive?

Just to make sure I don't miss you –
And heavens, that's something I'd dread –
To make sure I can recognise you
Will you wear a carnation?' she said . . .

Clive Webster

Never Been Kissed

Thirteen years old
And never been kissed
By Sarah or Sally
(I'll just check my list)

By Sophie or Becky
Or Shanti or Sharon
But have been kissed, just once,
By Darren.

(Well, we were practising!)

Roger Stevens

Lunch Break

He bought two beefburgers,
Egg, beans and chips,
Roll and butter, can of Coke.

I chose ham salad,
Diet lemonade, no bread.

He wolfed his down,
Swigged his Coke noisily.

I ate my food daintily,
Sipped my drink slowly.

He fetched some spotted dick
Floating in custard.

I chose an apple,
Green, 40 calories.

He looked at my plate.
I looked at his.

'I guess we're incompatible,' he said,
And split.

Pam Gidney

Barnsley

The first time
I was kissed,
     properly, I mean,
         and not scratched on the cheek
             by an aunt with a beard,
was in Barnsley.

She was thirteen,
     innocent
         and slim,
and, believe it or not, so was I.

Our lips met –

         It was in the bumper car
         at the fair.

Our lips parted –

         It was dark, the ride over,
         and her mum and dad
         could not
         see us.
         And neither could
         mine.

Our breathing deepened with passion –
         The man who took the
               money
         moved purposefully
         towards us.

Our hearts beat as one –
         and our orthodontic braces
            embraced.

I. R. Eric Petrie

My Mate Fancies You

My mate fancies you.

I don't fancy your mate
But my mate fancies your mate.

My mate doesn't fancy your mate
Cos my mate fancies you.

My mate's best mate fancies your mate's best mate.

My mate's best mate doesn't fancy your mate's best mate
My mate's best mate fancies your best mate.

My best mate doesn't fancy your best mate at all.
My best mate fancies your best mate's mate.

Oh . . . my best mate's mate
Doesn't fancy your best mate.
My best mate's mate fancies your best mate's best mate.

My best mate's best mate (which should be me but isn't)
Doesn't fancy your best mate
But my best mate's best mate
Fancies your best mate's best mate
(which should be you but isn't . . .)

Well . . . my best mate's best mate
Fancies your mate's best mate's mate.
Not your best mate's best mate.

I don't think my mate's best mate's mate
Is too keen on your best mate's best mate
Because my mate's best mate's mate
Fancies your best mate's mate's best mate.

That's no good . . . my best mate's mate's best mate
Fancies your mate's best mate's mate's best mate.

But my mate's best mate's mate's best mate
Fancies your mate.

But my mate fancies you.

I'll tell you what I fancy . . .

What?

A bag of chips. Do you?

Okay.

Paul Cookson

63

Turn that Racket Down

Paul Cookson

Turn that racket down! Are you going deaf?
Turn that racket down! It all the sounds the same!
Turn that racket down! Do you call that music?
Turn that racket down! It's driving me insane!

Have you ever used your hairbrush as a microphone? Do you fancy yourself as a bit of rapper? Can you play electric guitar? Do you annoy your parents by practising all these things at the same time . . . at full volume? If so, why not Rock and Roll along to this poptastic collection of poems chosen by Paul Cookson. 1 . . . 2 . . . a 1, 2, 3, 4

£2.99   0099417553